Let's Imagine What We Can Be

By: Kathleen Morgan

illustrated by: Amber Michaela Matthews

ibbilanepress.com

ISBN | 978-0-578-73004-2

I dedicate this book in loving memory of
my late husband, E. David Morgan, MD,
to my beautiful children and grandchildren
and to Gina, my writing coach, who all
gave me inspiration and encouragement
to pursue my dreams.

KM

David and Owen are brothers who really like to explore.
After their chores they run real fast to the great outdoors.

Soon they are climbing trees, grabbing branches and playing in the leaves.

As they are jumping around, they hear a whimpering sound.
They stop and see a tiny dog...stuck under a log!

They help the pup and set him free
and David and Owen are filled with glee...

Maybe when we grow up, we can take care of animals like that pup! Animal doctors or vets they are called...

They really do take care of them all. Cats, birds, lizards too, being a vet is a cool thing to do. Maybe one day that's what we could be

The next day arrives, we imagine something new
"We could build something fun, that's what we could do"
Soon they begin hunting for sticks...
Then put together something after finding some bricks
"We could build a factory or a tower up high,
Or a nice house, people could buy,

"We can make buildings as far as you can see.
An architect or engineer, maybe someday we'll be."

Other times we play army all day long.

Marching as soldiers' brave and strong
As we parade up and down, we hold our flags high.
Then imitate pilots flying planes in the sky.

Being in the military is very important indeed.
It keeps our country safe and our people free.

Another day we make believe we are actors on a stage,
where you can dance and sing and perform at any age.

Our imagination keeps us thinking of other things to do.
There are so many choices for me and you.
Let us imagine together what we could be.
The possibilities are endless as you can see...

A policeman keeps us safe day and night.

A teacher helps us all to read and write.

A computer tech is full of useful information.

Or maybe you could be president of our great nation.

Doctors and nurses take care of people everyday.

There are also sports you could play. You could play hockey,

or be a jockey.

Baseball, football, no matter your team.
Just go for it, whatever you dream.

Here is something we think about a lot;
Maybe we could be an astronaut?

We could fly into space and see all the stars.
Maybe we could also see Mars.

This is what mom and dad say to me,
"It doesn't matter what you imagine to be,

just know to be happy is the key.

You may have to work hard and go to special schools,
and listen to your teachers and follow certain rules.

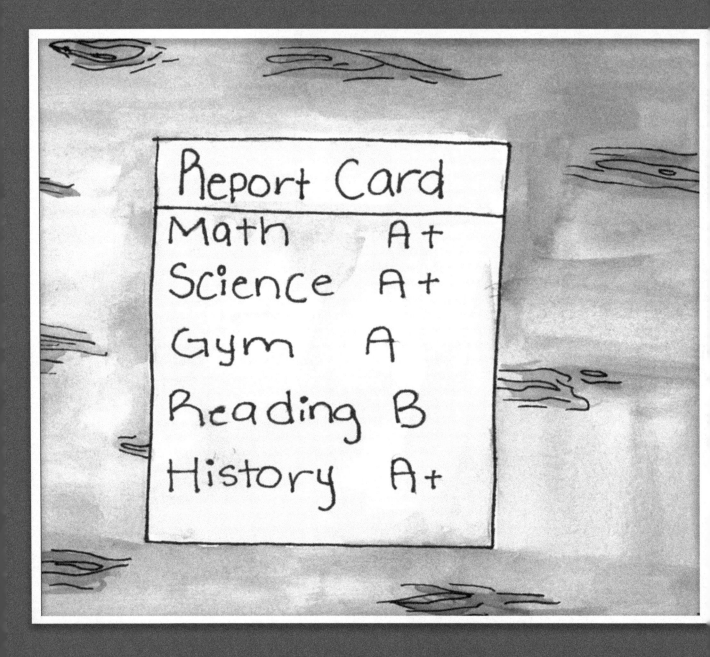

You will be taking many tests and hard exams, but always get the best grades that you can. Don't quit, give it all that you've got Keep on going and study a lot."

Reaching your dreams may take time. The road to the top is quite a climb. Be the person you want to be,

Then you will discover...hey that's me! So good luck to all, may your dreams come true. Become a special person...YOU!!!

CPSIA information can be obtained
at www.ICGtesting.com
Printed in the USA
BVHW021749300720
585068BV00015B/183

9 780578 730042